Active Learning for Catholic Kids

Reproducibles for Primary Grades
Volume I

Knowing the Catholic Church

Living by God's Rules

Caring for God's Creation

Stories From the Bible

PfLAUM
PUBLISHING GROUP

Dayton, OH

Using the CD-ROM

The CD-ROM that is enclosed with this book contains all the activities, each in an individual PDF file. You will need Adobe® Reader® to open and print these files. If you do not have Adobe Reader on your computer, you may download it free at www.adobe.com. Once you have Adobe Reader, simply insert the CD-ROM into your computer's CD-ROM drive and double-click on the file that bears the page number and name of the activity you want. You can then read the file and print as many copies as you need of the activity.

Activities by Jean Buell, Francine M. O'Connor, and Carole Essenmacher
Edited by Jean Larkin and Mary C. Noschang
Cover design by Matt Cole
Interior design by Linda Becker and Patricia Lynch
Production by Mario Ybarbo

Pflaum Publishing Group
2621 Dryden Rd., Suite 300
Dayton, OH 45439
800-543-4383
www.pflaum.com
ISBN 978-1-933178-83-7

Knowing the Catholic Church

Living by God's Rules

Caring for God's Creation

Stories From the Bible

Solutions to Selected Activities

Classy Quilt

God made each person special and wonderful. That includes you! Your identity comes from many things: your name, appearance, family, activities, interests, and beliefs.

This is your square for a classroom quilt. Follow the directions inside of it. Use lots of color! Cut out the square and glue it onto colored paper. After all the squares are taped together, your class will have a beautiful quilt!

Talk with your classmates about who you are, both as individuals and as a class. What makes each of you different? What makes you all the same?

My family:

↑
My
favorite food:

My
favorite animal:
↓

This is me:

My name is_____

My
favorite activity:
↓

My
favorite color:
↓

My church is_____

I believe in
    God the Creator,
    Jesus, God's son,
    the Holy Spirit.

Tradition... Tradition!

Name _____

Sometimes, people join groups. Each group, such as a family, a scout troop, or a church has its own "identity," which means that the members of the group may all do the same activities or believe in the same things. Groups with different identities can learn from each other.

Traditions are the ways that groups celebrate, week after week or year after year. Our families and our churches have many traditions that help us express what we believe. They help us learn who we are.

Color this Holy Water font. Where is it found?

_____

Who uses Holy Water?

_____

Draw a turkey dinner. What celebration is this?

_____

Who celebrates this holiday?

_____

Decorate this tree. What celebration does it show?

_____

Who celebrates this holiday?

_____

Draw candles on a cake for you. What celebration does it show?

_____

What do candles tell about you?

_____

"Well-come" Everyone!

Name_____

We are all invited to join God's family. We join this family in the sacrament of Baptism, when we promise to love God and to live in a way that pleases God. The priest blesses us with holy water. The water is kept in a large container that looks like a tall basin or a small pool. This container is called a baptismal font. Read about Jesus' Baptism in Matthew 3:13-17.

What does a baptismal font look like? Connect the drops to see an example.

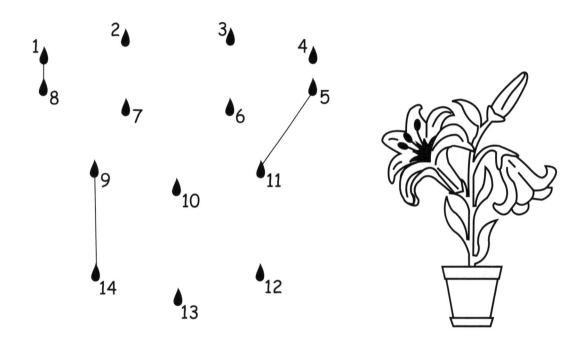

Have you ever dipped your fingers into holy water? How does water make you feel? How do you think God wants you to feel? Put the correct vowel (a,e,i,o,u) in the big drops below to find four words to describe how water makes us feel.

cl △ △ ns △ d   pl △ yf △ l

r △ fr △ sh △ d   en △ rg △ z △ d

Hear
Their Stories

God speaks to us through sacred stories. We hear them when we celebrate the Eucharist. We also hear prayers. The stories and prayers are read from special books. Have you ever seen them? Do you know what they are called?

Read the "story" that each book tells here. To find out the names of the books, follow the lines from each letter and write that letter in the blank box.

Look for me on a stand called the lectern.
Listen to my Bible stories during Mass.
Pray the Responsorial Psalm with me.
I am one of triplets. We tell different stories.
We take turns every three years.

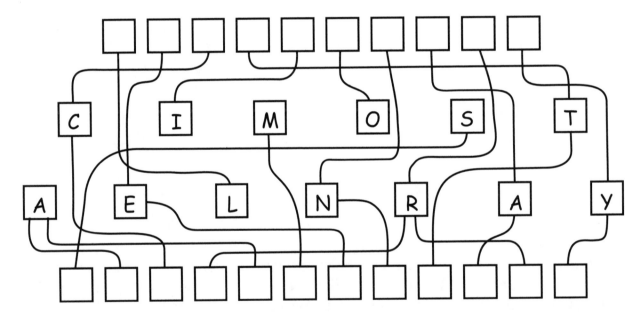

Look for me on a table called the altar.
Pray along as the priest reads my prayers.
Watch my calendar for holy days and feasts.
Honor the saints with my special prayers.
Follow my directions for special blessings.

Set the Table

Name_____

Jesus feeds us. We celebrate this gift in the sacrament of Eucharist. Eucharist means thanksgiving. Our celebration is a holy meal of thanksgiving. Read about a special meal that Jesus served in Luke 22:14-20. What special meals does your family serve?

Special dishes are used to serve our eucharistic meal. What are their names? On the lines below, write the letters that come before the letters given. Then draw a line from each answer to its picture. Color the pictures.

1. The holy meal is served from this special table.

____ ____ ____ ____ ____
 b   m   u   b   s

2. The special table is covered with this.

____ ____ ____ ____ ____   ____ ____ ____ ____ ____
 b   m   u   b   s   d   m   p   u   i

3. This cup contains the wine.

____ ____ ____ ____ ____ ____ ____
 d   i   b   m   j   d   f

4. This plate holds the bread.

____ ____ ____ ____ ____
 q   b   u   f   o

5. These containers hold the water and wine.

____ ____ ____ ____ ____ ____
 d   s   v   f   u   t

6. This covered container holds the Eucharist.

____ ____ ____ ____ ____ ____ ____ ____
 d   j   c   p   s   j   v   n

a b c d e f g h i j k l m n o p q r s t u v w x y z

Prepare the Meal

We celebrate the gift of Jesus in the sacrament of Eucharist. After our holy meal of thanksgiving, we respect the Real Presence of Jesus.

Use these words to fill in the blanks below.

Afterward   altar   bread   ciborium   Eucharist
everyone   lighted   nourishes   Real   The

_____ priest stands at the
_____. He prays and blesses the
_____ and wine. They become the Holy
_____, the body and blood, the
_____ Presence of Jesus. Jesus
_____ us when we receive Holy Communion.
_____, the Holy Eucharist is put in a
_____. It is stored in a special cabinet. A
_____ candle called a "sanctuary light" shows
_____ that Jesus is present.

What is the name of the special cabinet? Write the first letter of each line.

—— —— —— —— —— —— —— —— —— ——

We respect the Real Presence of Jesus. We genuflect when we walk past the tabernacle. That means to stop walking, kneel on one knee, and stand up again. These pictures show you how. Practice in class!

1. Stand.   **2. Kneel on one knee.**   **3. Stand.**

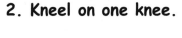

Open the Door

God forgives us. Always. We celebrate this with the sacrament of Reconciliation. It usually takes place inside a small room called a "reconciliation room." Have you ever opened the door? What symbols of God's love are inside?

Look inside this doorway. Lightly color in a checkerboard pattern, using two different colors. Read the words of each color to find messages about forgiveness.

We	The	pray
door	with	to
the	God's	priest.
love	God	is
forgives	open	our
to	sins.	you!

Read a story about reconciliation in Luke 15:11-24.

Celebration Clothes (page 1)

When we celebrate, we often celebrate with special clothes, such as a new Easter outfit. Our clothes can also mean something special in our relationship with God.

1. At baptism, we are given a white garment. This shows our new life in Christ. Do you have a white baptismal garment at home? Some babies wear a white garment that was worn by their parents and grandparents when they were baptized.

2. At first Eucharist, some girls wear white dresses, and some boys wear white shirts. White clothing shows that we have been baptized. Have you received your first Eucharist? If you have, draw your clothing on one of the figures above. If you haven't, draw what you would like to wear. Show that you have been baptized!

Celebration Clothes (page 2)

3. Many priests wear clothing like this. Notice the collar. It shows that he is a priest. Color his outfit black or gray.

4. The priest wears vestments to celebrate Mass. First, he puts on an alb to show that he is baptized. Albs are white. They can be worn by any baptized person who leads prayer.

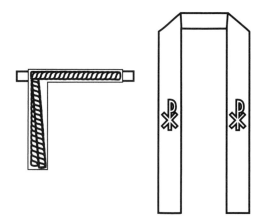

5. Next the priest puts on a belt that is made of rope. It is called a cincture. Then he puts a stole on his shoulders. This shows that he is a priest. (A deacon wears a stole over only one shoulder.) Color this stole the color for this liturgical season.

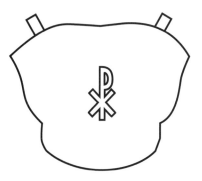

6. Finally, he puts on a chasuble. Decorate this chasuble for a celebration. Use the same color as the stole. Now cut out the pictures and show how a priest gets ready to celebrate Mass!

Signed and Sealed

Name_____

We believe in God. We show this with the "Sign of the Cross." We say, "In the name of the Father, and of the Son, and of the Holy Spirit. Amen." We trace a big cross onto ourselves. It is a little prayer with a big meaning.

What does the Sign of the Cross say about our faith? Use the code to fill in the blanks. Then read about the BIG meaning of this little prayer. Practice making the Sign of the Cross.

Code:

1. We _____ in God. Our God is the Blessed Trinity:

Our Creator; Jesus, the Son; and the Holy Spirit.

2. We _____ in God's life. We are baptized!

3. We _____from Jesus. We follow him.

4. We _____ whenever we love. Jesus gives us hope.

5. We _____God's help. The Holy Spirit guides us.

Hand in Hand

Name_____

We pray in many ways, even with actions. Action-prayers are called "gestures." What gestures have you noticed? A handshake is one. Long ago, people shook hands to show they did not have weapons. We still shake hands to greet each other. It is a sign of love. The priest invites us to shake hands. He reminds us of words that Jesus said.

Find out what Jesus said. Write the names of the pictures. Afterward, say them all together and listen carefully. Then write the real words that Jesus used.

   U,

_____ _____ _____ _____

M+   2 U.

_____ _____ _____ _____ _____ _____ _____

Solve this puzzle, too. Find out what we say when we shake hands in church. Practice in class. Keep your hand firm. Look at each other's eyes when you say the words.

  -C U.

_____ _____ _____ _____

Love Glows On

Name_____

God always loves us. God's family is called the "communion of saints." It includes people who have died. They continue to love us, and we continue to love them. We remember them by lighting candles called "votive lights." Have you ever lit one?

Do you know people who have died? They share everlasting life with Jesus. "Light" candles for them by coloring a flame for each one. Tell who they are.

1. work
   rest
   labor

2. us
   we
   them

3. light
   dark
   dim

4. shine
   dull
   dingy

5. eyes
   ears
   souls

6. lying
   faithful
   disloyal

7. upset
   peace
   unrest

8. dispute
   disagree
   Amen

Each candle has three words. Circle the word that means something different from the others. Write it on the correct line below. Then say this prayer for your loved ones who have died.

Eternal _____ grant to _____, O Lord,
          1   2
and let perpetual _____ _____ upon them.
                       3   4
May their _____, and all the souls of the
               5
_____ departed, rest in _____. _____ .
      6   7   8

At Your Fingertips

Name_____

Mary was the mother of Jesus. Now she is in heaven. We can ask her to help us. We can pray the "rosary." When we pray the rosary, we hold a string of beads. The beads help us keep track of the prayers. Have you ever held a rosary?

Learn to pray the rosary. Add vowels (a, e, i, o, u) to form the "Hail Mary." Practice reading it. Each time you practice, color a small bead on this rosary. Start at the cross and work your way around the loop. When you come to a large bead, say what you know of the Lord's Prayer. Use a ball point pen and press really hard when you color the beads! You will be able to feel the beads on the other side of the paper. Then you can practice from memory!

The Hail Mary

H__i l M__ry, f__ll __f gr__ce, th__
L__rd __s w__th yo__. Bl__ssed __re
yo__ __mong w__men, __nd bl__ssed
__s th__ fr__it __f y__ur w__mb,
J__sus. H__ly M__ry, m__ther __f
G__d, pr__y f__r __s s__nners n__w,
__nd __t th__ ho__r __f o__r d__ath.
Am__n.

Follow the "Cross Walk"

Name_____

Jesus suffered and died. We recall this when we pray the "Stations of the Cross." Look for 14 pictures along a wall in your church. These are the "stations." They show what happened when Jesus walked with his cross. We imagine we are walking with him.

These pictures show the stations. The titles tell what is happening in each one. Draw a line to match each picture with its title. What do you feel when you see what happened to Jesus? How are you like the people along the way? How are you different?

Jesus Falls the Second Time

Jesus Accepts His Cross

Jesus Dies on the Cross

Simon Helps Jesus

Jesus Is Taken Down from the Cross

Jesus Speaks to the Women

Jesus Is Condemned to Death

Veronica Wipes the Face of Jesus

Jesus' Clothes Are Taken Away

Jesus Is Laid in the Tomb

Jesus Is Nailed to the Cross

Jesus Falls the Third Time

Jesus Falls the First Time

Jesus Meets His Mother

Design
a Shrine

Saints are people who lived holy lives. Now they share eternal life with God. "Statues" and "shrines" help us remember who they were and how they lived. They help us to live holy lives, too. Which saints have statues in your church?

Make a shrine. Choose a saint who can help you. Write the saint's name inside. Decorate the shrine with symbols that remind you to love others. Cut it out and glue it to colored paper. Hang it in your bedroom. Ask your saint to help you every day.

Seeing Is Hearing

Name_____

God speaks to us through the sacred stories in the Bible. Long ago, most people could not read. Bible stories were told with pictures in "stained glass windows." People looked at the pictures. They prayed about the stories. Then they could hear God speak to them! Are there any stained glass pictures in your church?

Follow the number code, and color the picture below. What Bible story do you think this tells? When do you see this story happen at Mass? Read Matthew 14:13-21.

1. Blue	4. Yellow	7. Green
2. Gold	5. White	8. Red
3. Brown	6. Gray	9. Orange

A-maze-ing Incense!

Name_____

God hears our prayers. Sometimes, we use "incense" while we pray. Incense is a mixture of perfumes and spices. When it is sprinkled over hot coals, it makes smoke. The smoke rises toward the sky. We imagine our prayers rising too. Have you ever smelled incense? Can you pray with your nose?

The smoke coming out of this censer is really a maze! Start at the coals and find a path to the top. Then go back and copy the letters into the spaces below. They form a prayer to say whenever you see or smell incense. You can pray with your nose!

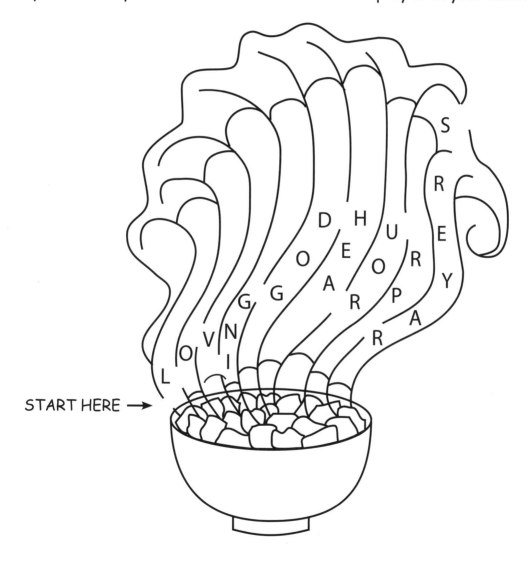

START HERE →

_ _ _ _ _ _ _   _ _ _ ,   _ _ _ _ _   _ _ _   _ _ _ _ _ _ _ _!

Cross of Love

Name_____

Jesus died on a cross. Then he rose to new life. Someday, we will rise to new life, too. Have you noticed the cross in your church? The cross is an important symbol of our faith. It reminds us that it's not always easy to love as Jesus did. Crosses also remind us that Jesus always loves us. He teaches us, he heals us, and he helps us to love.

On this cross, write words or draw pictures that show the ways that Jesus loves you.

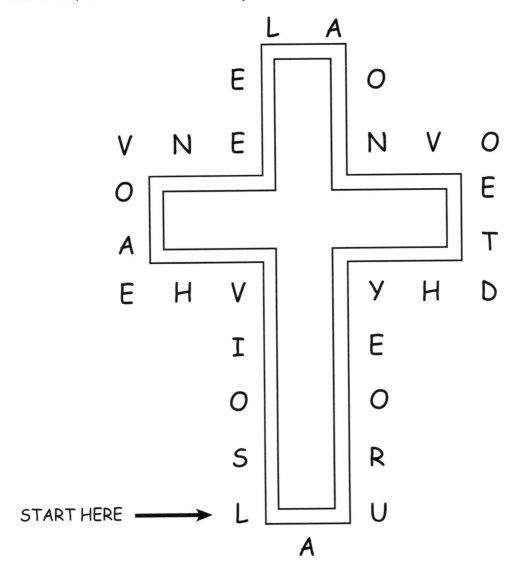

Write down the letter that the arrow points to. Moving clockwise, skip a letter and write down the next. Continue until you reveal a special message from Jesus to you!

__ __ __ __ __   __ __ __   __ __ __ __ __ __   __ __ __ __   __ __ __

__ __ __ __ __   __ __ __ __ __   __ __ __ .

Light of Life

Name_____

Jesus is the Light of the world. What symbol reminds us? Find two words in the top row of letters. Write them here.

_____ _____

Have you seen this symbol in your church? It's tall, isn't it! Follow these directions to make a small picture of it.

1. Find the "B's." Color them with black.

2. Find the "O's." Color them orange.

3. Find the letters that spell "cross." Color them red. This reminds us that Jesus died before he rose to new life.

4. Find empty spaces below the cross. Write the year that it is right now. This tells how long it's been since Jesus died.

5. Look beneath the cross. Find an "A" and an upside-down "U." Circle them with blue. They are the first and last letters of the Greek alphabet. This reminds us that Jesus is the beginning and the end of all things.

Jesus' light shines for all of us. We can share his light by loving others. Look near the orange letters. Circle 6 words that show how you can share Jesus' light with others today. They are in all directions. Write them below.

```
E A S T E R : C A N D L E
A A X A L L E L U I A X A
L U I A X A L L E L U I A
K L L E L U I A X A L L E
L N L L E L M U I A U R X
E X A L L E S L U I A S X
L E A H L L O E L H U I A
U I A X T O O O S A L E L
I A X A O O O O O L L U L
Y A R P O O O O O C A R E
C L I A O O O O O X A L L
H L X A L O O O H L E L U
R E A B X A O L L E L U I
I L L B B L O A L E L I A
S U L B : B B L I A X P L
T I E B : : : B B L A L L
I A L B : : : : : B L A E
S L U B : : : : : B L L L
T L I B : : : : : B E L U
H E A B : : C : : B L E I
E L L B : : R : : B U L A
L U L B C R O S S B I U H
I I E B : : S : : B A I E
G A L B : : S : : B L A I
H L U B : : : : : B L L S
T L I B : : A : : B E L R
A E A B : : Ω : : B L E I
M L L B : : : : : B U L S
E U L B         B I U E
N I E B : : : : : B A I N
```

1. P_____   2. T_____   3. S_____

4. S_____   5. C_____   6. H_____

A Time to Serve

We are all called to love God and to love one another. We answer God's call in different ways. Some people answer God's call by making special promises. They promise to love God and to serve God's people. They are "priests," "deacons," and "sisters." Do you know any priests, deacons, or sisters?

Find out some ways that priests, deacons, sisters, and others spend their time serving God and God's people. Use this clock. Find the letters on the hours for the times that are given. Write them in the blanks. Draw lines to show who does what. More than one line can go to each person.

1. ___ ___ ___ Mass.
   9:00 1:00 12:00

2. ___ ___ ___ ___ ___ ___ at Mass.
   1:00 9:00 9:00 5:00 9:00 10:00

3. ___ ___ ___ ___ ___ people who are sick.
   11:00 5:00 9:00 5:00 10:00

4. ___ ___ ___ ___ people who are poor.
   4:00 3:00 6:00 7:00

5. ___ ___ ___ ___ ___ children.
   10:00 3:00 1:00 2:00 4:00

6. ___ ___ ___ ___ people who ask for guidance.
   4:00 3:00 6:00 7:00

7. ___ ___ ___ ___ ___ ___ the parish council.
   1:00 9:00 9:00 5:00 9:00 10:00

8. ___ ___ ___ ___ other jobs besides the Church.
   4:00 1:00 11:00 3:00

9. ___ ___ ___ ___ throughout the day.
   7:00 8:00 1:00 12:00

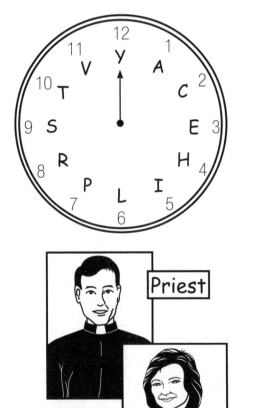

Many, Many Ministers

Name_____

Jesus reminds us of the two greatest commandments: to love God and to love one another. Some people follow these commandments by serving the people who come to Mass. They are called "ministers." How many ministers have you noticed?

Look below. Read about many, many ministers. Then circle the underlined words.

```
E U C H A R I S T I C G
B L H N I B N L D H O R
N D O N U T S E C C M E
A J S B M E T I H D M E
E L P E V E R Y O N E T
M E I A P L U D I S N E
I C T R U H M O R I T R
N T A E Q P E F T E A S
I O L R L V N G I F T S
S R I S A N T Q R E O F
T U T E R C A N T O R P
E S Y G L H L E A D E R
R H V E S T I B U L E I
S E R V E R S R O T M E
A R Y L H O T C I R T S
B S A C R I S T A N N T
```

Before you arrive, the <u>sacristan</u> is busy preparing the worship space. <u>Greeters</u> meet you as soon as you walk in, and <u>ushers</u> help you find a place to sit. The <u>minister</u> for Children's Liturgy of the Word helps you reflect on the readings while the <u>lector</u> proclaims the Word, the <u>priest</u> proclaims the Gospel, and the <u>commentator</u> reads the petitions. The <u>cantor</u> and <u>choir</u> help you sing your prayer, and the <u>instrumentalists</u> help everyone sound good. The gift <u>bearers</u> represent the community when they present the bread and wine. <u>Eucharistic</u> ministers distribute Holy Communion. All during Mass, the <u>servers</u> help, too. After Mass, look at the pamphlets in the <u>vestibule</u>. You might find a way to share your <u>gifts</u> through ministry. <u>Everyone</u> can minister to one another. It can be as simple as showing our <u>hospitality</u> by sharing a greeting or, perhaps, some <u>donuts</u>!

"Linked" to the Apostles

The apostles knew Jesus very well. They shared their faith with people who continued to share their faith through many, many years. Now, we share it, too. Our faith is linked to the apostles! We state our beliefs in a prayer called the "Apostles' Creed."

Here are statements of the Creed. Cut them apart. Keep them in order and make a "paper chain" to take home. Snip off one link each day and memorize what it says.

1. We believe God the Father created heaven and earth.
2. Jesus is God's son, our Lord.
3. Jesus was conceived by the Holy Spirit and born of the Virgin Mary.
4. Jesus suffered, was crucified, died, and was buried.
5. He rose again on the third day and ascended to the Father.
6. He will come again to judge us.
7. We believe in the Holy Spirit and the Holy Catholic Church.
8. We believe in the communion of saints and the forgiveness of sins.
9. We believe in the resurrection of the dead and the life everlasting.

Name _____

The Happiness Poster

1. **I am the LORD, your God; you shall not have strange Gods before me.**
Remember how much God loves you. Put God first in your life.

2. **You shall not take the name of the LORD your God in vain.**
God's name is holy. Say it with love.

3. **Remember to keep holy the LORD's Day.**
Sunday is the Lord's Day. Go to Mass and do good deeds.

4. **Honor your father and your mother.**
Love and obey your parents.

5. **You shall not kill.**
Be gentle. Never hurt others.

6. **You shall not commit adultery.**
Show respect for the gift of your body. Respect others.

7. **You shall not steal.**
Respect what belongs to others.
Do not take or damage what belongs to others.

8. **You shall not bear false witness against your neighbor.**
Tell the truth about others. Tell the truth about everything.

9. **You shall not covet your neighbor's wife.**
10. **You shall not covet your neighbor's goods.**
Be thankful for what you have. Do not be jealous of what others have.

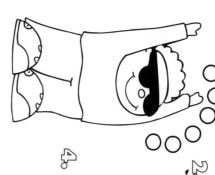
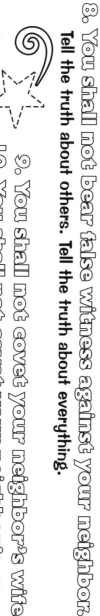

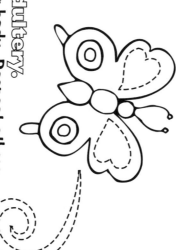

Moses, Man of God

Name _____

Moses was chosen by God to lead the Hebrew people out of Egypt. The people followed God through the wilderness. God sent them quail, and every morning but the Sabbath they found cakes of bread called *manna* on the ground to eat.

But God's people were not happy. They mumbled and they grumbled.

Moses didn't know what to do, so he put on his coat and climbed a high mountain to talk to God.

God gave Moses two stones with ten rules written on them. They were God's ten rules for happiness. Solve the **Circle Quote** to learn what we call God's rules. Begin at the arrow and write down every other letter on the blanks below. You will go around the circle two times.

Circle Quote

Start here.

The __ __ __

__ __ __ __ __ __ __ __ __ __ __ __

Loving God Always

Name _____

1 Put God first in all you do.

2 Say God's name with love.

3 Always keep God's day holy.

The first three commandments are about loving God every minute of every day of your life. You must never forget them.

Complete these sentences by filling in the blanks from the Word List.

Word List

AFRAID	FRIENDS
BIBLE	GIFTS
CHURCH	LISTEN
COMMANDMENTS	THANK YOU
DECISIONS	PRAYERS

1. Remember to say your __ __ __ __ __ __ __.

2. __ __ __ __ __ __ to God's Word.

3. Read the __ __ __ __ __.

4. Go to __ __ __ __ __ __ with your family.

5. Obey the __ __ __ __ __ __ __ __ __ __ __ __.

6. Tell your __ __ __ __ __ __ __ __ about God.

7. Don't forget to say __ __ __ __ __ __ __ __ to God.

8. Turn to God when you are __ __ __ __ __ __.

9. Ask God to help you make __ __ __ __ __ __ __ __ __.

10. Enjoy the trees and flowers and other __ __ __ __ __ of God.

Three More Ways to Love God

Name _____

Jesus tells us we should love God with our whole heart, with our whole soul, and with our whole mind. What does this mean?

You love with your whole HEART when you have warm, loving, and caring feelings about someone. You don't feel angry or jealous, just kind and gentle. You want to do good things for this person. This is the way God loves you. This is the way you can love God with all your heart.

You love with your whole MIND when you always think nice things about your loved one. When you pray, you are loving God with your mind. When you think about God, you are loving God with your mind. God thinks about you all the time. You can love God like that too.

You love with your whole SOUL when your loved one becomes a part of everything you say and do. When you have an important decision to make, you talk it over with your loved one and decide on what is best for both of you. This is the way God loves you. You can love God like that too.

I will love God with my whole heart by _____

I will love God with my whole soul by _____

I will love God with my whole mind by _____

Finish these sentences in your own words.

Which Commandment?

Name _____

Sin is a failure to love God. One of the ways we sin is by breaking one of God's Ten Commandments. Sin causes us to be unhappy, and it causes the people in our lives to be unhappy too.

Show how we can change our unhappiness to happiness by drawing a line from each sin to one of God's Ten Commandments.

Sin ☹ ⟶ ☺ Commandment

1. Steal a candy bar. ☹

2. Disobey your parents. ☹

3. Hit someone in anger. ☹

4. Refuse to go to Sunday Mass. ☹

5. Blame your sister for something you did yourself. ☹

6. Be jealous of your friend's new bike. ☹

☺ a. Honor your father and your mother.
Love and obey your parents.

☺ b. You shall not kill.
Be gentle. Never hurt others.

☺ c. You shall not steal.
Respect what belongs to others. Do not take or damage what belongs to others.

☺ d. You shall not bear false witness.
Tell the truth about others.
Tell the truth about everything.

☺ e. You shall not covet your neighbor's goods.
Be thankful for what you have.
Do not be jealous of what others have.

☺ f. Remember to keep holy the LORD's Day.
Sunday is the Lord's Day.
Go to Mass and do good deeds.

Write a prayer telling God you are sorry for any time you have broken a commandment.

Dear God, _____

_____

_____

_____

Which Is the Greatest?

One day some people asked Jesus which commandment was the greatest. Read the story in the Bible in Matthew 22:34-38. Then find Jesus' answer hidden in the puzzle below. Use the key to decipher the message.

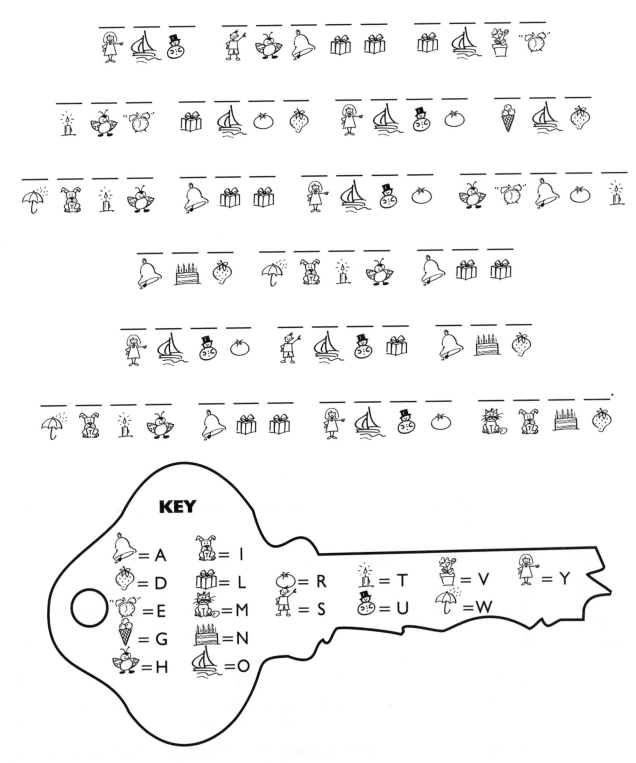

A Circle of Love

Name _____

How do you love others with a perfect love? Just follow Jesus' way of love!
To see what that is, decode the message below. Begin at the arrow and
read every other letter until you have gone around the circle two times.
Write the letters in the blanks below the circle. (If you need help, go to
your Bible and read John 13:34.)

Start here.

"JUST __ __ __ __ __ __ __ __ __ __ __ __ __ __ __ __,

YOU SHOULD ALSO LOVE ONE ANOTHER."

In the center of the **Circle of Love**, you will find several ways that Jesus
loves us. How can you follow his example in those ways?

_____

_____

Ways to Love Others

Name _____

We know that Jesus loved us in many ways. We also know that Jesus wants us to love others as he has loved us.

COMFORT
I will imitate Jesus' comforting care by

_____

_____

FORGIVE
I will imitate Jesus' forgiveness by

_____

_____

TEACH
I will remember the stories of Jesus and follow him by

_____

_____

GUIDE
I will learn Jesus' rules and follow his example by

_____

_____

HELP
Jesus always helped those in need. I will follow his example by

_____

_____

LOVE
I will follow the lesson Jesus taught me about love by

_____

_____

Sermon on the Mount

Name _____

Read about the Beatitudes in Matthew 5:3-9. Do you know what they mean?

- If you are *poor in spirit,* God is more valuable to you than anything in the world.
- If you are *meek and gentle,* you let others have their way when they are right.
- If you are *merciful,* you have a forgiving nature.
- If you *mourn,* you are sad because someone you love has died.

- If you *hunger for righteousness,* you want everyone to follow God's way.
- If you are *pure in heart,* you want only things that are good or right.
- If you are a *peacemaker,* you seek peace and try to find ways to keep others from fighting.

Now finish each sentence by choosing the correct word from the list.
Use your Bible if you want to take another look at Matthew 5:3-9.

Blessed are...

1. Blessed are the poor in spirit, for theirs is the kingdom of _____.

2. Blessed are those who mourn, for they will be _____.

3. Blessed are the meek, for they will inherit the _____.

4. Blessed are those who hunger and thirst for righteousness,

   for they will be _____.

5. Blessed are the merciful, for they will receive _____.

6. Blessed are the pure in heart, for they will see _____.

7. Blessed are the peacemakers, for they will be called

   _____ of God.

Word List
filled • children • earth • comforted • God • heaven • mercy

What It Means to Be Blessed

Name _____

What does it mean to be blessed? According to Jesus, being blessed does not mean being rich or being smart or being beautiful or popular. Being blessed means more than all these things put together. Being blessed means loving God more than anything in this world and being loved by God in a very special way.

Solve the acrostic puzzle to learn the wonderful thing about being blessed. Fill in the answers to the Picture Clues. Then put each letter in its numbered space in the Jesus quote.

Picture Clues

___ ___ ___ ___
13 2 22 17

___ ___ ___
20 15 24

___ ___ ___ ___ ___
 6   8 23   9

___ ___ ___ ___
11 14 10 12

___ ___ ___ ___
 3   19   1

___ ___ ___
    18   5

___ ___ ___ ___
 7   16   21

___ ___ ___
    4   25

Jesus told the people, "Rejoice and be glad, for...

___ ___ ___ ___   ___ ___ ___ ___ ___ ___   ___ ___   ___ ___ ___ ___ ___
 1   2   3   4   5   6   7   8   9 10   11 12   13 14 15 16 17

___ ___   ___ ___ ___ ___ ___ ___ ___ ." (Matthew 5:12)
18 19   20 21 22 23 24 25

Yes or No?

We choose to be blessed when we say *Yes* to loving one another as Jesus loved us. We also can choose to say *No*, and then we refuse the blessing.

In each story below, someone has a choice to say Yes or No to being blessed. There are two endings to each story. After reading each ending, decide if the person chose Yes or No to God's blessing. Put a check in the box that shows your answer.

1. Eduardo is very good in math. Talisha is not. Eduardo got an A+ on his math test. Talisha got a D. Eduardo feels happy and proud. Talisha feels disappointed and sad.

Eduardo laughs at Talisha and calls her a dummy.

YES ❑   NO ❑

Eduardo offers to help Talisha study for the next test.

YES ❑   NO ❑

2. The family who lives down the street from Amy is having a hard time. The father is sick and the mother was laid off from her job. The children have a few toys, but they are mostly broken. Amy's mother asks Amy to share her toys with the children.

Amy says the children are careless and will probably just break the toys, so she won't give them any of hers.

YES ❑   NO ❑

Amy takes some toys to the children and teaches them some new games.

YES ❑   NO ❑

3. Shawn and Casey are playing catch. The little boy next door wants to play with them. He is only three and doesn't know how to catch a ball very well yet.

They tell him he's too small to play catch and send him home.

YES ❑   NO ❑

They say okay and they try to teach him how to catch the ball.

YES ❑   NO ❑

A Chance to Choose

Name _____

In Chapter 4 of Matthew's Gospel, we read that when Jesus was in the desert, Satan came to him and tried to talk him into doing wrong. Sometimes we hear tempting words from others who want us to do wrong.

Each sentence in the crossword clues is a temptation to do wrong, to commit a sin. The names of the sins are all confused and scrambled, just like we feel sometimes when we are tempted. Solve the crossword by unscrambling the sins and writing them into the puzzle.

TEMPTATIONS

SINS

ACROSS

3. If you lean over, you can read the answers on Mary's paper.

CEHATNIG _____

4. Go ahead, take the candy bar. The store will never miss it.

SATENILG _____

5. Bobby's being a big jerk. He deserves to get smacked.

AGERN _____

DOWN

1. So what if your parents said no? They're not here now, are they?

DSIBOEDNIECE _____

2. Hide the pieces so your mom won't know you broke her vase.

LNGYI _____

Taking the Right Path

Can you find your way through this maze to the place where Jesus waits for you?
Watch out for the temptations along the way.

The Perfect World Puzzle

Name _____

What if everyone in the world followed God's rules? What do you think would be missing from our world then?

Cut out each piece of The Perfect World puzzle. Then see if you can put together a perfect world.

A Special Bonus

Whenever someone came to Jesus in need, he was always ready to help them. As you set out to follow Jesus, your first step will be to help those who need you. When you do this, Jesus tells you that something special happens. Do you know what that special thing is?

Solve the code-word puzzle, using the key below. See what Jesus tells you about the things you do for others.

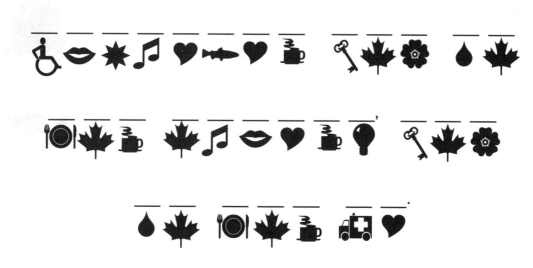

W H A T E V E R   Y O U   D O

F O R   O T H E R S'   Y O U

D O   F O R   M E.

✴ = A		🍵 = R
💧 = D		💡 = S
♥ = E		🎵 = T
🍽 = F		🌸 = U
👄 = H		➤ = V
🚑 = M		♿ = W
🍁 = O		🗝 = Y

Doing Good

Name _____

The Church imitates Jesus by performing the Corporal Works of Mercy. To discover how our Church serves the people of God, match the works of mercy with their proper signs of Christian love.

a.

Haven for the Homeless

b.

Corporal Works of Mercy

1. Feed the hungry.

2. Give drink to the thirsty.

3. Clothe the naked.

4. Visit the imprisoned.

5. Shelter the homeless.

6. Visit the sick.

7. Bury the dead.

e.

f.

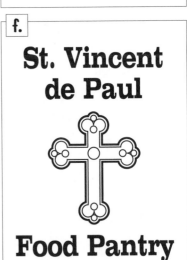

c.

d.

g.

Name _____

Praying for Others

Jesus wants us to care about others—not just about their bodies but also about their souls. The Church has many ways to help people to grow in spirit. These are called the Spiritual Works of Mercy.

Use the Key to decode the seven works of mercy listed here. Replace all 1's with A's, all 2's with B's, and so on.

Key

1=A	6=F	11=L	15=P	19=U
2=B	7=G	12=M	16=R	20=V
3=C	8=H	13=N	17=S	21=W
4=D	9=I	13=N	17=S	22=Y
4=D	9=I	14=O	18=T	
5=E	10=J			

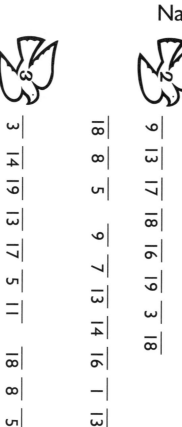

1. 3 14 / 3 14 13 20 5 16 18 / 17 9 13 13 5 16 / 18 8 5

2. 9 13 / 17 18 16 19 3 18 / 5 9 7 13 14 16 1 13 18 / 16 18 / 8 5 18

3. 3 / 14 19 13 17 5 11 / 18 8 5 / 4 14 19 2 18 6 19 11 / 18 8 5

4. 17 / 14 16 16 14 21 / 3 14 12 6 14 16 18 / 18 8 5 / 6 19 11 / 18 8 5

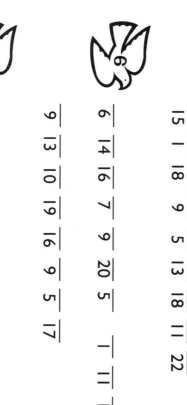

5. 2 5 1 16 / 5 1 16 / 21 16 14 13 7 17 / 18 9 5 13 18 11 22 / 16 1 18 9 5 13 18 11 22

6. 6 14 16 7 9 20 5 / 14 16 7 9 16 / 1 11 11 / 19 16 9 16 / 14 6 6 5 13 17 5 17 / 5 5 17

7. 15 16 1 22 / 16 1 22 / 6 14 16 / 18 8 5 / 11 9 20 9 13 7 / 1 13 4 / 4 5 1 4 / 13 7 4

Playing Fair

Name _____

Playing fair means being as honest with others as we want them to be with us. It means not always having to be first or best. You will always play fair as long as you do what Jesus said.

Using the Word List below, find each word in the puzzle. Then put the words together in the sentence to see the advice Jesus gave us about playing fair. (Clue: one word is hidden inside another word!)

Word List

AS

BE

EVERYONE

TO

TREAT

TREATED

WANT

YOU

E	S	B	L	X	C	O	T
H	V	O	G	B	E	I	R
R	D	E	P	T	K	D	E
V	T	R	R	A	T	E	A
L	R	Q	C	Y	M	U	T
W	A	N	T	K	O	B	E
N	G	L	J	Y	H	N	D
A	S	V	H	F	M	I	E

T _ _ _ _   E _ _ _ _ _ _ _   A _

Y _ _   W _ _ _

T _   B _   T _ _ _ _ _ _ .

Fairness Flower

Make a fairness flower to keep in your room to remind you that Jesus wants you to follow the Golden Rule and treat others fairly at all times.

Cut out the patterns on the dotted lines. Trace one flower center and as many petals and leaves as you want onto construction paper. You can use green paper for the leaves and other pretty colors for the flower's center and petals. On the flower center, write the word FAIRNESS. On each petal, write a special time, place, or activity for acting fairly. Some ideas are listed. You can use these or think of some of your own.

Paste a stem made from a green pipe cleaner in the center of another sheet of construction paper. Paste the flower leaves along the stem. Then paste the flower center and each petal in place.

Hang your Fairness Flower where you can see it often as a reminder always to play fair.

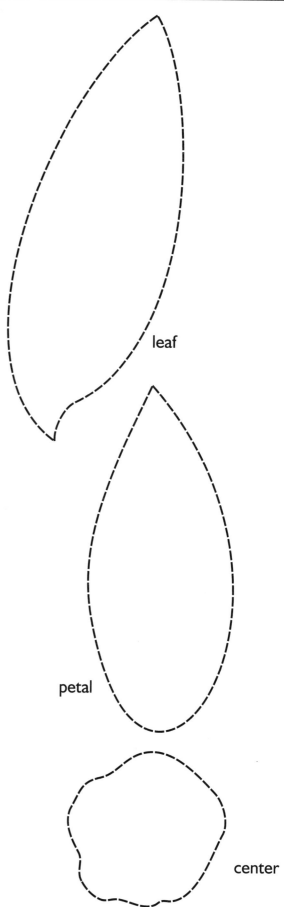

leaf

petal

center

Fixing the Circle of Love

When one person hurts another person's feelings or does something wrong to that person, a friendship ends, and the circle of love is broken. You can make things right and repair the circle.

Fill in the correct word to complete the sentences in the circle slices. Then cut out the slices and make a poster by pasting the slices into a circle shape on construction paper. Your poster will help you remember what to do if you are unkind to someone and need to repair the Circle of Love.

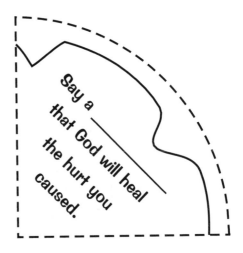

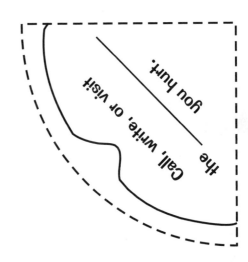

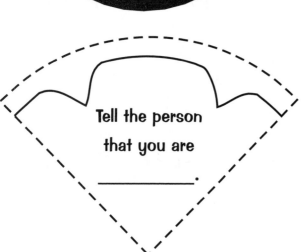

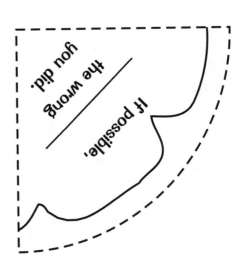

Be a Peacemaker

Name _____

The word *peacemaker* is made up of two words—*peace* and *maker*. You can be a peacemaker by finding ways to help people love one another. At Mass, we wish our friends and neighbors a special kind of peace. Solve the acrostic to discover what we call the special peace that comes from Jesus.

$\overline{}_{2}\ \overline{}_{5}\ \overline{}_{6}\ \overline{}_{16}\ \overline{}_{11}$

$\overline{}_{10}\ \overline{}_{9}\ \overline{}_{15}\ \overline{}_{1}$

$\overline{}_{10}\ \overline{}_{6}\ \overline{}_{7}\ \overline{}_{13}$

$\overline{}_{17}\ \overline{}_{15}\ \overline{}_{14}\ \overline{}_{14}\ \overline{}_{6}\ \overline{}_{16}$

$\overline{}_{7}\ \overline{}_{9}\ \overline{}_{10}\ \overline{}_{10}\ \overline{}_{8}\ \overline{}_{3}$

$\overline{}_{4}\ \overline{}_{5}\ \overline{}_{6}\ \overline{}_{7}\ \overline{}_{12}$

$\overline{}_{1}\ \overline{}_{2}\ \overline{}_{3}\ \ \overline{}_{4}\ \overline{}_{5}\ \overline{}_{6}\ \overline{}_{7}\ \overline{}_{8}\ \ \overline{}_{9}\ \overline{}_{10}\ \ \overline{}_{11}\ \overline{}_{12}\ \overline{}_{13}\ \ \overline{}_{14}\ \overline{}_{15}\ \overline{}_{16}\ \overline{}_{17}$

Now, just for fun, see how many words you can make from the letters in the word *peacemaker*. A few have been done for you.

PEACEMAKER

cream   cape

Two Special Sacraments

Name _____

Jesus comes to us in two special sacraments that help us to follow him and to make our world a better place. Solve the two rebus puzzles below to discover what Jesus gives us in each of these sacraments.

This is a special gift we receive from Jesus in the Sacrament of Reconciliation.

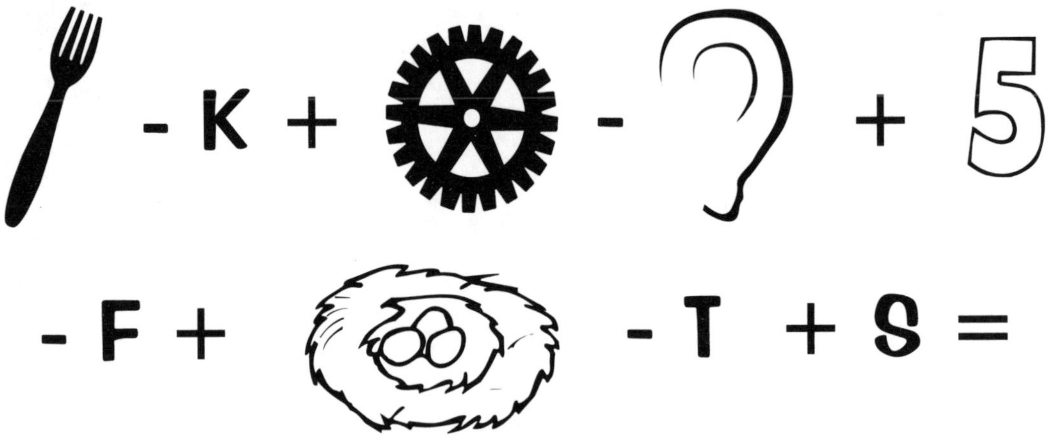

− K + − + 5

− F + − T + S =

_____
Use this line to work on.

_____
Write your solution here.

In the Sacrament of the Eucharist, Jesus makes us one with our Christian brothers and sisters. The rebus will tell you another name for that oneness.

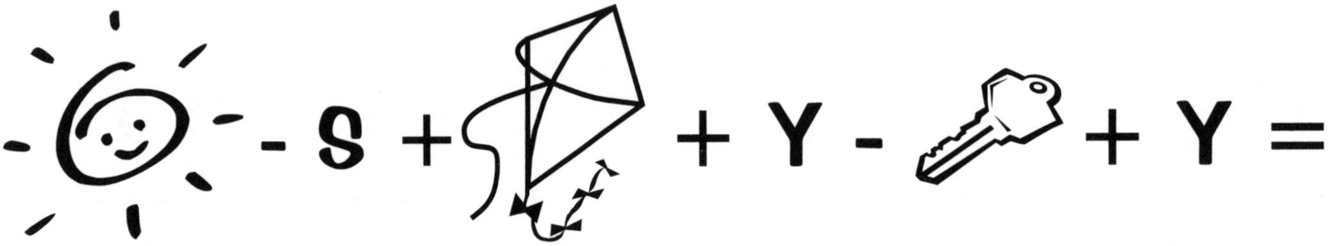

− S + + Y − + Y =

_____
Use this line to work on.

_____
Write your solution here.

God Created the Heavens and the Earth
Genesis 1:1-13

Name _____

First Day: Day and Night

In the beginning, everything was dark, and God said, "Let there be light." God called the light *day*.

Part of the time it was dark. God called the darkness *night*.

And God was pleased.

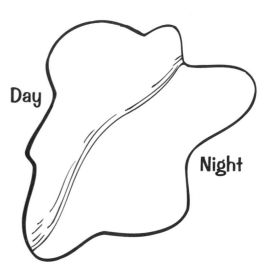

Color day white.
Color night black.

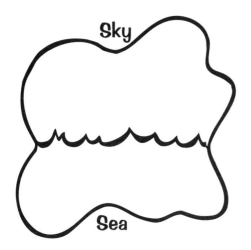

Second Day: the Heavens and Sea

On the second day, God created the crystal clear waters of the oceans, lakes, and rivers.

Then God made the bright blue sky. God called the sky *heaven* and the waters *sea*.

And God was pleased.

Color sky light blue.
Color sea dark blue.

Third Day: Earth and Vegetation

On the third day, God made the land and covered the ground with seeds that grew into beautiful plants and trees. God called the land *earth*.

And God was pleased.

Color land, grass, flowers, and trees.

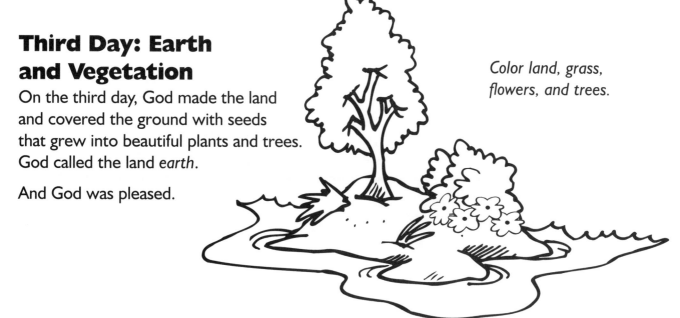

And Everything Within

Genesis 1:14-31

Name _____

Fourth Day: Heavenly Bodies

On the fourth day, God made the two great lights— the sun to guide the day, and the moon and stars to guide the night. And God was pleased.

Fifth Day: Birds and Fish

On the fifth day, God made the birds that filled the skies and the fish and other sea creatures to fill the seas, lakes, and rivers. And God was pleased.

Sixth Day: Animals and People

On the sixth day, God made all the animals to roam the forests, plains, and jungles. Then God made people. And God was pleased.

Color this page. Then draw a line from the pictures at the bottom of the page to the place where each belongs. Or, cut out the figures at the bottom and paste each one where it belongs.

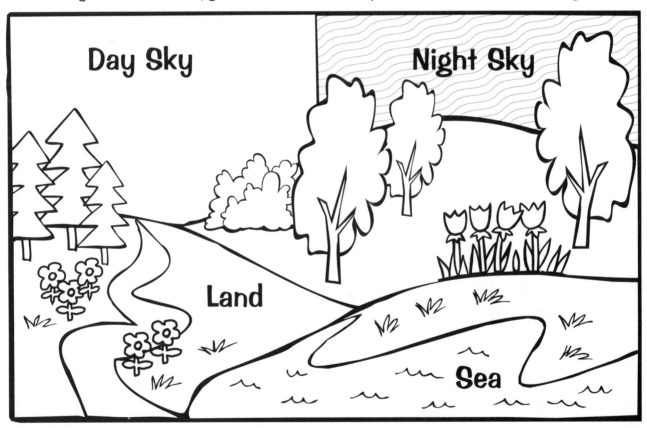

A Day of Rest
Genesis 2:1-4

Name _____

On the seventh day, God was finished with the creation. So God blessed the seventh day and rested from all the work that had been done.

The wonder and beauty of God's creation is all around us.

Draw your favorite animal.
God created it.

Draw one of your favorite people.
God created this person.

Draw your favorite tree.
God created it.

Draw your favorite fruit.
God created it.

We Grow in God's Love
Genesis 1:26-30

God made all the people and blessed each and every one. God created people out of the earth and called them children of God. We are all special to God no matter what we look like, where we are, or what we do.

God made families to love and care for one another. Write the names of your family members on each apple. Then color the apples and tree. Add more apples if needed.

Name _____

My Family Tree

God's Loving Creation   Name _____
Psalm 145:8-16

God loves and cares for all of creation: The forests, the flowers, the animals, the mountains, the waters, sea creatures, and, most of all, God loves people. God's love of this beautiful creation is everlasting.

Using the letter code below, finish the poem:

God made the _____ and _____ _____

God made the _____ that _____ us _____

God made the _____ that swim the _____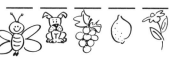

God made the _____ that sing in the _____

God made the _____ large and small,

And God made _____ . God _____

= A		= S		= V		= M
= E		= N		= L		= moon
= I		= G		= R		= stars
= U		= H		= T		= sun
= O		= fish		= birds		= Y

Creation
Word Search

Genesis 1:31

Circle all the words that tell about God's creation.

Word List

AIR
CLOUDS
DOGS
EARTH
ELEPHANTS
FISH
FLOWER
HEAVENS
MOON
PEOPLE
RABBITS
STARS
SUN
TREES
WATER
WIND

```
D O S T R A M T B C I E Z E F
H F I S H J L O P Q X L Z D R
R S U U V B F G O R W E T E A
A D E N G I T J L N M P N O P
P E O P L E A R T V F H B C H
U W B G J L T H E A R A V Z Q
R P A O Q J T V H E I N L O P
A C I R T R F G W H S T A R S
B Y R P A S V O X I Y S Z D A
B U Z E E C L O U D S G N H J
I L D K D F A L W F Z I A L A
T M O P M Q N T V C W B O I P
S K G D W A T E R Q R S W Y E
F G S O S U T J H E A V E N S
```

Take a walk and look for other good things God has made. Make a list.

All Living Creatures
Genesis 1:28-31

Name _____

When God made people, God asked them to take care of all the creation: the fish of the sea, the birds in the sky, and every living thing that moves. God gave us seeds to grow food, wood and clay to build houses, and cotton and wool for us to make clothes. God's plan provided homes, food, and clothing for the other living creatures.

Below are places that some of God's creatures use for their homes. Draw a line from the creature to its home. You can also draw in other creatures that use these places for homes.

THERE'S NO PLACE LIKE HOME!

WELCOME!

Home, Sweet Home

fish

bird

rabbit

Answer the following questions by filling in the blanks with one of the three animals pictured above.

Who wears feathers for clothes?

_____

Who wears fur for clothes?

_____

Who wears scales for clothes?

_____

Who eats carrots and grass?

_____

Who eats seeds and bugs?

_____

Who eats water plants and water bugs?

_____

God's Plan for Us
Luke 10:27

God has a wonderful plan for us. We are to love God and to share our love with others.

Circle the words in this list that are ways of showing our love for God and for others.

Sharing

Forgiving

Helping

Hitting

Being kind

Stealing

Loving

Praying

Lying

Now color and decorate the picture, then cut it out and tape it around a clean can (one without sharp edges). Fill the can with paper or real flowers and give it to someone who needs your love.

Name _____

Smile, God Loves You

A Sad Story (page 1)
Genesis 2:4—3:24

Name _____

In the beginning the earth was beautiful with blue lakes,
clean air, and green lands filled with animals, plants and trees.
Then God made people, and they
were to respect creation and take good care of it.
But many of those people were careless and did not respect God's work.

The people put poisons
and other junk in the blue lakes.
These things killed the fish
and other water life.

The people littered the lands with garbage
and cut down the trees,
leaving the land bare and lifeless.
This destroyed the place where animals lived.

The people burned poisons
and built cars and factories
that made smoke, which turned
the air dark and thick.

The people made bombs and other weapons
to kill other people.

When people do not respect
God's beautiful creation,
the plants and animals, the sky
and the seas—and the people—all suffer
and are often destroyed forever.

These are all very sad things and
are not part of God's plan.

A Sad Story (page 2)

Name _____

Finish the sentences to tell what people have done to harm God's beautiful creation. Refer to the story on page 1 if you need to check your answers.

Careless people have:

1. _____ the lands with garbage.

2. put _____ and _____ in the blue lakes.

3. _____ the fish and other water life.

4. _____ too many trees.

5. destroyed the place where many animals _____.

6. filled the air with _____.

7. made many _____ to kill people.

8. shown _____ for God's creation.

9. These are sad things and are not part of God's _____.

Word List

killed
smoke
poisons
lived
cut down
weapons
disrepect
plan
littered
junk

What's Wrong?

Job 33:4

God gave us life by making the air we breathe. All people, animals, and plants need clean air to breathe.

God gave us water, which all living things also need. We cannot live without clean water.

Look at the pictures below and see if you can figure out what is wrong with each one. Write the correct caption under each picture.

Name _____

Captions

Dirty water kills animals and plants.

Water not safe for swimming.

Water not safe for drinking.

Heavy smog. Air not safe to breathe.

I Can Help

Name _____

Fill in the blanks with words from the list below.

I can help keep the water on God's beautiful earth clean and

safe by **s**_____ water. I will remember to

t_____**o**_____ water when I am not using it and to

take brief **s**_____ instead of baths. I will keep

lakes, rivers, and beaches clean by picking up **l**_____.

And if I see someone **p**_____ the lakes and

streams, I will report that person to an adult whom I trust.

I can help keep the air on God's beautiful earth clean and

safe by remembering to **c**_____ on things that put

s_____ into the air, such as heaters and cars. I will

w_____ or use a bike when possible instead of

r_____ in a car. I will put on a sweater instead of

turning the **h**_____ up. If I see someone who is causing

p_____ in the air, I will report that person to an

adult whom I trust.

Word List

conserve (save)	showers	saving	pollution	riding	smoke
turn off	poisoning	litter	walk	heat	

A Walk in the Forest   Name _____

Cut out the cards below and shuffle them. Place them upside down next to the animal print game board. Play the game with a friend. Use a coin, stone, or button for a marker. Draw a card and follow the directions on the card. When you use up all the cards, shuffle them and continue the game.

Land left bare causes mud slide. Go back one space.		
Rainforest cleared of all living things. Lose 2 turns.	Planted trees. Move ahead 1 space.	Move 1 space.
Burning trash sets forest fire. Lose one turn.	Planted flowers and gardens. Take another turn.	Move 1 space.
Trees cut for newspapers. Forest is dead. Lose one turn.	Recycled newspapers. Move 2 spaces.	Move 2 spaces.
Trees cut for people's homes. Go back two spaces.	Used cloth instead of paper. Move 1 space.	Move 3 spaces.

Saving the Trees

Many trees are used to make newspapers and other paper products, so we need to **conserve** (use as little as possible) and **recycle** (use things more than once).

Did you know that if everyone in the United States recycled Sunday newspapers it could save more than 500,000 trees every week?

Trees are used to build homes, and land is cleared of all the plants to make room for homes and businesses. Not only are trees and plants necessary for food and as homes for animals, but green plants make oxygen, which people and animals need to breathe.

Solve the following word puzzle using the letter code to find out what you can do to save the forests.

1 = A	5 = E	9 = O	13 = T
2 = B	6 = G	10 = P	14 = U
3 = C	7 = L	11 = R	15 = W
4 = D	8 = N	12 = S	16 = Y

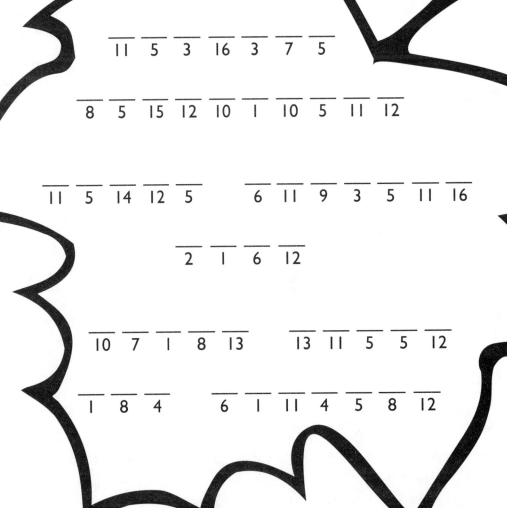

$\overline{11}\ \overline{5}\ \overline{3}\ \overline{16}\ \overline{3}\ \overline{7}\ \overline{5}$

$\overline{8}\ \overline{5}\ \overline{15}\ \overline{12}\ \overline{10}\ \overline{1}\ \overline{10}\ \overline{5}\ \overline{11}\ \overline{12}$

$\overline{11}\ \overline{5}\ \overline{14}\ \overline{12}\ \overline{5}\quad \overline{6}\ \overline{11}\ \overline{9}\ \overline{3}\ \overline{5}\ \overline{11}\ \overline{16}$

$\overline{2}\ \overline{1}\ \overline{6}\ \overline{12}$

$\overline{10}\ \overline{7}\ \overline{1}\ \overline{8}\ \overline{13}\quad \overline{13}\ \overline{11}\ \overline{5}\ \overline{5}\ \overline{12}$

$\overline{1}\ \overline{8}\ \overline{4}\quad \overline{6}\ \overline{1}\ \overline{11}\ \overline{4}\ \overline{5}\ \overline{8}\ \overline{12}$

How We Can Save the Animals

Cut on dotted line.

Which of God's creatures lives in here?

Fold open door on solid line.

Read Luke 12:6

This book belongs to _____

Be Kind to Pets

Report animal abuse to parents, teachers, or clergy.

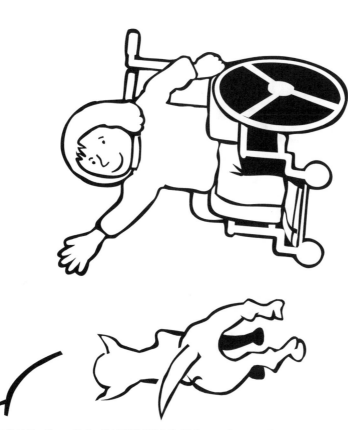

Psalm 148:9

Remember that God is good to all, and God's tender care rests on all the creatures.

PRAY: Dear Lord, make us true friends to all animals so that we might protect all of your creation.

4

Take Care of the Food Source for Wild Animals

Build feeders for the birds and wildlife.

Plant a garden.

Keep a bird bath full of fresh water.

Plant special gardens for wildlife with wild grasses and grains. Get a book at your library that describes the wildlife in your area and what they eat.

Don't Pollute

Talk to adults about helping to keep poisons, bug sprays, oil, weed killer, and other pollutants out of the air, water, and ground.

2

Take Care of Wild Animals' Homes

Build bird houses.

Plant trees, gardens, and shrubs.

Hundreds of thousands of animals live in the forests, jungles, and grasslands. Yet people keep cutting trees, clearing the land, and leaving the animals homeless.

You can help by writing letters to the newspapers and talking to adults who can help.

3

Our Bodies
Praise God

Name _____

Draw a line to each part of the body described in the poem below.

God gave me to see the earth,

My to fold in prayer.

God made my to say kind words

To people everywhere.

God gave me to hear the birds.

Whose songs are pure and fair.

God made my **L** for smells so sweet

Of flowers in the air.

I want to use my head and heart,

To serve the world with love.

I'll try to use these all for good,

To praise my God above.

Saying No to Bad Habits

Name _____

When we disobey God and abuse our bodies with harmful drugs and other things, that is a very sad thing. God wants us to be healthy. What can we do to keep ourselves healthy?

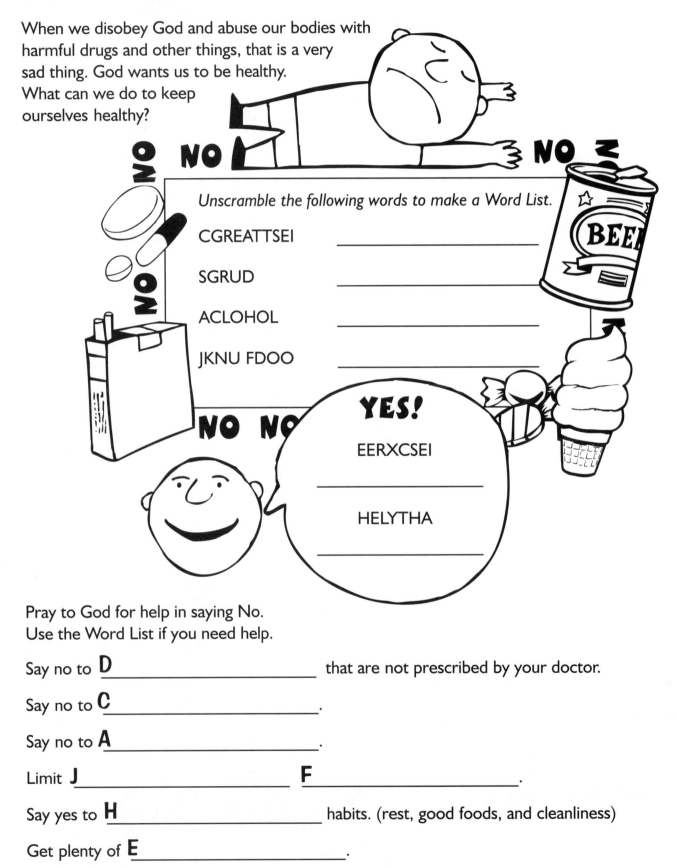

Unscramble the following words to make a Word List.

CGREATTSEI   _____

SGRUD   _____

ACLOHOL   _____

JKNU FDOO   _____

YES!

EERXCSEI

_____

HELYTHA

_____

Pray to God for help in saying No.
Use the Word List if you need help.

Say no to **D**_____ that are not prescribed by your doctor.

Say no to **C**_____.

Say no to **A**_____.

Limit **J**_____ **F**_____.

Say yes to **H**_____ habits. (rest, good foods, and cleanliness)

Get plenty of **E**_____.

Love One Another
John 4:7

God wants us to love and respect all people, those of all colors and religions and those who are disabled, troubled, elderly, and sick. God even asks that we love and respect our enemies.

Write the following sentences in the correct columns.

Are kind and polite to all people.

Use words that hurt others.

Steal from others.

Want others to be happy.

Forgive those who make mistakes.

Lie and cheat to get our own way.

Share what we have with others.

Use words that are kind.

Are unkind and rude to others.

Don't care about other people.

We show respect when we:

1. _____

_____

2. _____

_____

3. _____

_____

4. _____

_____

5. _____

_____

We show disrespect when we:

1. _____

_____

2. _____

_____

3. _____

_____

4. _____

_____

5. _____

_____

Caring for God's Creation

Name _____

Read Psalm 8. Then solve the Word Search puzzle below.

ALUMINUM
CARING
CREATION
ECOLOGY
ENERGY
ENVIRONMENT
GARBAGE
GLASS
GOD'S WORLD
HELP
LITTER
PAPER
PLASTIC
POLLUTION
RECYCLE
REUSE
SAVE
STEWARDSHIP
TREES
WATER

Peace Poem
Matthew 5:9

Name _____

God wants all of creation to live together in peace, and God is the source of that peace. Only through the love of God and our love of God's creation can we find that peace.

Here are directions for how to write a poem, called a *cinquain*, about God's peace. For additional ideas, read Psalm 29:11, Psalm 133, and 1 Corinthians 13.

The first line is written for you. It is one word: *Love* (the source of peace).

On line two, write two words that describe love to you (patient, gentle, kind, never ending).

On line three, write three words that tell something about what love does (forgives, blesses, cares for others, lasts forever).

On line four, write four words that tell how you feel about love and peace (happy, not afraid, peaceful).

On line five, write one word that could also mean love (peace).

love

_____ _____

_____ _____ _____

_____ _____ _____ _____

_____

Thank You, God

Name _____

Read Psalm 104. Then read the prayer below. Color and cut out this prayer and hang it in your room to help you remember to thank God for the wonders of creation and of God's everlasting love.

PRAYER OF THANKSGIVING

Thank you, God, for the beauty and glory of your creation.

Thank you for the gifts of walking and running, for the beauty of the earth, for the wind and the rain, for the sound of a newborn baby.

Thank you for the beauty of the sun, moon, stars, rainbows, trees, flowers, and all the wonderful creatures that share this earth with us.

Thank you for your everlasting love and forgiveness.

Help us to remember to care for this wonderful earth and all the animals, plants, air, water, ourselves, and one another.

Amen

Mary and the Angel

Name _____

The Annunciation (Luke 1:26-38)

The angel Gabriel came to Mary with a very important message. Can you decode the angel's message and Mary's answer? The key is listed below.

Angel's Message

__ __ __ __   __ __ __ __

__ __ __ __   __ __ __

__ __ __ __   __ __ __ __

__ __ __ __

__ __ __ __

__ __ __ __ __ .

Mary's Answer

_ __ __ __ __ __   __

__ __   __ __   __

__ __ __ __   __

__ __ .

Key

$\quad$ = A $\qquad$ = I $\qquad$ = O

$\quad$ = D $\qquad$ = J $\qquad$ = S

$\quad$ = E $\qquad$ = K $\qquad$ = U

$\quad$ = F $\qquad$ = L $\qquad$ = V

$\quad$ = G $\qquad$ = M $\qquad$ = W

$\quad$ = H $\qquad$ = N $\qquad$ = Y

Jesus Is Born
The Nativity (Luke 2:1-7)

Name _____

Read the story of the birth of Jesus in the Bible. Then solve the crossword puzzle.

Christmas Crossword

Word List

AUGUSTUS
BETHLEHEM
CHRISTMAS
DONKEY
HOLY FAMILY
INN
INNKEEPER
JOSEPH
MANGER
MARY
STABLE

Across

2. The town where Jesus was born.
4. A filled-up place, no room here for Jesus.
5. Birthday of Jesus
7. Jesus' mother
9. Mary rode on this.
10. Foster-father of Jesus
11. The building where Jesus was born.

Down

1. Jesus, Mary, and Joseph
3. Jesus' first crib
6. He turned Mary & Joseph away
8. Emperor who asked for a census

Messengers from Heaven
Angels and Shepherds (Luke 2:8-20)

Name _____

On the day that Jesus was born, angels appeared to some shepherds on the hill, singing and praising God. After you solve the acrostic puzzle, you will almost be able to hear the song that the angels are singing.

__ __ __ __ __
16 24 25 4 13

__ __ __ __
19 17 26 20

__ __ __ __ __
1 14 7 21 6

__ __ __ __ __
22 15 27 6 23

__ __ __
10 3 8

__ __ __ __
18 11 4 2

__ __ __ __ __
21 13 9 28 15

__ __ __ __
5 25 4 12

"__ __ __ __ __ __ __ __ __ __ __ __
  1 2 3 4 5 6 7 8 9 10 11 12

__ __ __ __ __ __ __ __ __ __ __ __ __ __ __ __ ."
13 14 15 16 17 18 19 20 21 22 23 24 25 26 27 28

Star Search (page 1)
The Magi (Matthew 2:1-12)

Name _____

Three kings followed the star of Bethlehem looking for Jesus, the newborn King. They came to honor him with gifts. Do you have a star who helps you to know Jesus? You might even have more than one. Maybe your star is your mother or your teacher or your Bible. Maybe it's all three plus others. How many "stars" (people or things that lead you to God) can you find and circle in the puzzle below?

A	E	I	F	M	T	L	S	G	C
U	P	R	A	Y	E	R	I	P	Q
A	M	O	T	H	E	R	S	D	X
E	K	O	H	Q	N	L	T	P	F
M	P	T	E	A	C	H	E	R	H
C	B	G	R	J	I	B	R	I	Z
Y	I	R	B	R	O	T	H	E	R
W	B	F	R	I	E	N	D	S	V
D	L	H	K	O	S	R	N	T	J
N	E	I	G	H	B	O	R	X	B

Word List

BIBLE	BROTHER	FATHER
FRIEND	MOTHER	NEIGHBOR
PRAYER	PRIEST	SISTER
	TEACHER	

Star Search (page 2)

Name _____

Cut out this star pattern and trace around it on construction paper.
Write your name on your star. Then write the names of all the stars
in your life—the people who help you know and love Jesus.

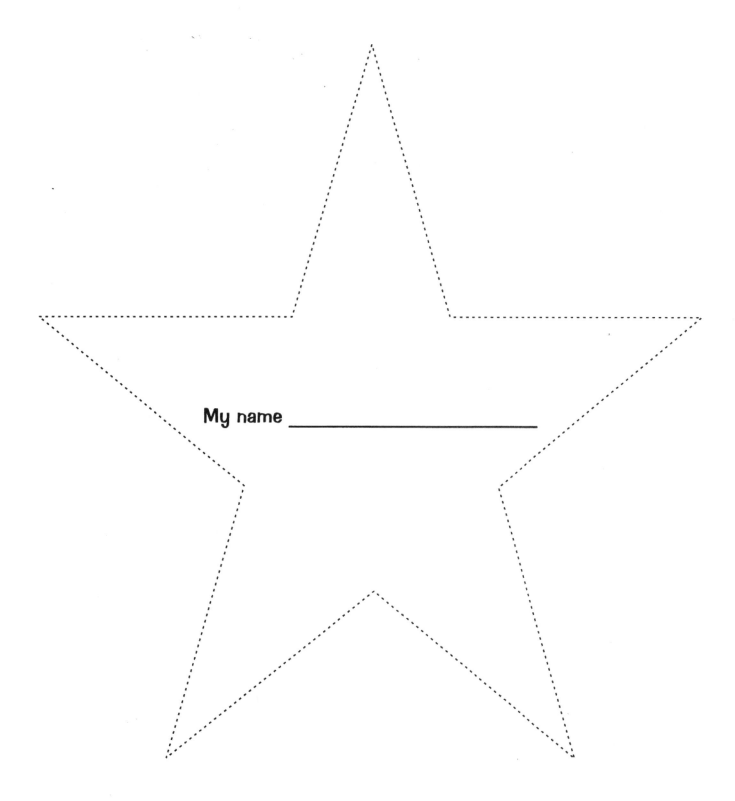

My name _____

Keeping Jesus Safe
The Flight to Egypt (Matthew 2:1-14)

Name _____

When Jesus was born, King Herod was the ruler of the land. He lived in Jerusalem. While the three wise men were following the star to Bethlehem, they stopped in Jerusalem and told King Herod they were searching for "the child who has been born king of the Jews."

When the king heard this, he was not happy. He didn't want any other kings in his land. He told the wise men to let him know where they found Jesus so that he could also go honor the new king. But he didn't really want to honor Jesus. He really planned to kill him.

After finding Jesus and paying him honor, the wise men were warned by an angel not to go back to Jerusalem and tell Herod where to find Jesus. An angel also appeared to Joseph in a dream and said, "Get up, take the child and his mother, and flee to Egypt, and remain there until I tell you; for Herod is about to search for the child, to destroy him."

Joseph and the wise men obeyed the angel. The wise men went home without going back through Jerusalem. Joseph took Mary and Jesus to Egypt, where they lived until after Herod died and it was safe to return to Nazareth.

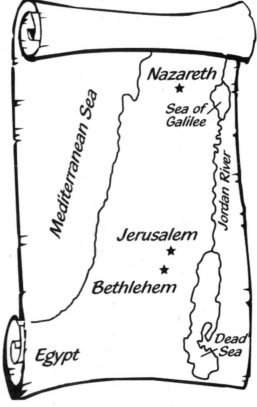

Word List

Jerusalem
King Herod
Nazareth
Bethlehem
The Wise Men
Egypt

Choose the correct word from the Word List to answer the questions below.

1. Who was the ruler of the land where Jesus was born? _____

2. In what city did the king live? _____

3. Who first told the king that Jesus had been born? _____

4. In what town was Jesus born? _____

5. Where did the angel tell Joseph to take Mary and Jesus? _____

6. After the king died, where did the Holy Family make their home? _____

Little Boy Lost

Name _____

Jesus in the Temple (Luke 2: 41-52)

When Jesus was twelve years old, he went with Mary and Joseph to Jerusalem. This was a journey the Holy Family took every year, for there was a holy festival, or party, going on in Jerusalem. When the festival was over and the family was on their way home with all the other people, Mary and Joseph noticed that Jesus was not with them. They returned to Jerusalem to look for him. After three days they found him in the Temple, sitting with the priests and teachers. Mary was upset and worried. As soon as she saw her son, she scolded him for worrying her.

Solve the acrostic and find out what Jesus said when Mary scolded him.

Clues

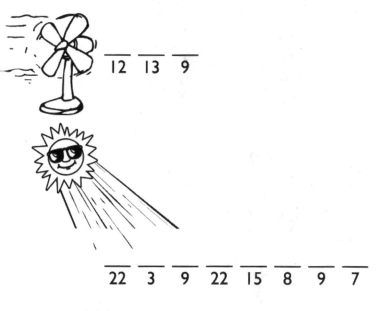

$\overline{12}\ \overline{13}\ \overline{9}$

$\overline{22}\ \overline{3}\ \overline{9}\ \overline{22}\ \overline{15}\ \overline{8}\ \overline{9}\ \overline{7}$

$\overline{5}\ \overline{19}\ \overline{21}\ \overline{10}\ \overline{6}$

$\overline{14}\ \overline{1}\ \overline{17}\ \overline{16}$

$\overline{14}\ \overline{20}\ \overline{11}\ \overline{4}$

$\overline{2}\ \overline{16}\ \overline{9}$

$\overline{6}\ \overline{16}\ \overline{23}\ \overline{18}$

Answer

Jesus said to Mary, "Did you not know...

$\overline{1}\quad \overline{2}\quad \overline{3}\quad \overline{4}\quad \overline{5}\quad \overline{6}\quad \overline{7}\quad \overline{8}\quad \overline{9}\quad \overline{10}\quad \overline{11}$

$\overline{12}\ \overline{13}\ \overline{14}\ \overline{15}\ \overline{16}\ \overline{17}\ \overline{18}\quad \overline{19}\ \overline{20}\ \overline{21}\ \overline{22}\ \overline{23}\,?"$

Something to think about...

Why do your parents want to know where you are at all times?
Have you ever been the cause of worry for your parents?

Jesus and the Devil
Temptation (Matthew 4:1-11)

Name _____

Read the gospel story above and see how hard the devil tried to make Jesus do something wrong. The devil is so good at tempting people that he is often called "the tempter." Sometimes the devil tempts us through our friends, sometimes by making wrong things look right, and sometimes just by making us want things we don't need. Write the letter or the correct answer on the line near the temptation.

1. "So what if your mother says we can't see that movie? Who's going to tell her?"

_____

2. "Nobody will notice if I just slip this candy bar into my pocket without paying."

_____

A. Stealing

B. Lying

C. Disobedience

D. Jealousy

E. Cheating

4. "Let's run! We'll say that Maury broke the window."

_____

3. "Mary's not looking right now, and I can see her paper. She's smart, so I'll just copy her test answers."

_____

5. "Angelina gets everything she wants. I hate her for getting that new bike I wanted."

_____

Do you know the words we say at the end of the Lord's Prayer to ask God's help during times of temptation? Write them here.

_____

_____

Naming the Twelve
The Apostles (Mark 3:13-19)

Name _____

To help him in his work of building God's Church, Jesus chose twelve men. After listening to the story of how Jesus chose each of these men, see if you can find and circle their names in the puzzle below.

```
A  M  E  I  M  Q  R  N  J  F  B
B  A  R  T  H  O  L  O  M  E  W
V  T  A  D  W  J  U  D  A  S  X
B  T  G  I  O  A  J  H  N  X  C
Q  H  J  U  A  M  B  V  D  T  R
W  E  U  C  P  E  T  E  R  X  J
S  W  D  Y  H  S  D  Z  E  T  O
K  N  A  S  I  M  O  N  W  L  H
T  Y  S  E  L  P  N  F  Z  U  N
L  P  S  O  I  J  A  M  E  S  K
D  H  G  C  P  T  H  O  M  A  S
```

ANDREW • BARTHOLOMEW • JAMES (Find 2)

JOHN • JUDAS (Find 2) • MATTHEW • PETER

PHILIP • SIMON • THOMAS

Bonus Questions

 Which apostle betrayed Jesus? _____

 Who was the first apostle named by Jesus? _____

⭐ Which apostles were brothers?

_____   _____

_____   _____

Jesus and the Children
Blessing (Mark 10:13-16)

One day, while Jesus was talking to the people, he told them something very special about children. Solve the acrostic to learn what Jesus said. To solve the puzzle, first write the answers to the picture clues. Then transfer the letters to the numbered blanks in the quote.

__ __ __ __
17 20 4 8

__ __ __ __
7 16 12 14

__ __ __ __ __
15 5 9 10 11

__ __ __ __
21 20 16 14

__ __ __ __
8 2 18 1

__ __ __ __ __
3 6 13 19 5

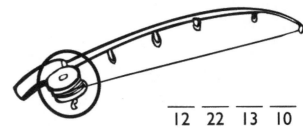

__ __ __ __
12 22 13 10

__ __ __   __ __ __
1 2 3   4 5 6

__ __ __ __ __ __ __ __
7 8 9 10 11 12 13 14

__ __ __ __
15 16 17 18

__ __   __ __.
19 20   21 22

Something to think about and discuss...

Can you name three ways you can "come to Jesus" this week?

1. _____

2. _____

3. _____

The Lesson at Cana
Miracle (John 2:1-11)

Name _____

Have you ever been to a wedding? This Bible story is all about a wedding in a town called Cana. When the wedding party ran out of wine, Mary told Jesus about it. Then she told the waiter to do something that we all should do.

Begin at the arrow and read every other letter around the circle to see what Mary told the waiter.

Start here.

___ ___   ___ ___ ___ ___   ___ ___ ___ ___

___ ___ ___ ___ ___   ___ ___ ___.

Something to think about...

Can you name three things that Jesus tells us to do? Write them here.

1. _____

2. _____

3. _____

Jesus Cures a Little Girl
Miracle (Luke 8:40-56)

Name _____

In the story of Jairus' little girl, Jesus brought good news to the family. To learn what this good news was, begin at the arrow, read every other letter around the "family circle," and transfer each letter to the blanks below the circle.

Start here.

__ __ __ __ __ __ __ __ __ __ __ __ ,

__ __ __ __ __ __ __ __ .

Look at these other times in the Bible when people were sad because someone had died and then were surprised by a miracle.

1. John 11:1-44

Who was sad?

_____

What was the surprising miracle?

_____

_____

2. Luke 7:11-17

Who was sad?

_____

What was the surprising miracle?

_____

_____

3. John 30:19-21

Who was sad?

_____

What was the surprising miracle?

_____

_____

Jesus Feeds the Hungry
Miracle (Matthew 14:13-21)

Name _____

Read the story of how Jesus fed thousands of hungry people. And there were even twelve baskets left over! You may not be able to feed the hungry in exactly the same way Jesus did, but you can help fight hunger today too.

On the baskets below are signs telling who you can help by giving food today. But the signs have gotten all mixed up. Can you unscramble the signs (using the Word List below)?

PROO

_____

HMOESELS

_____

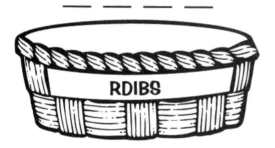

RDIBS

_____

SUTH-NIS

_____

DOOF NAPYRT

_____

YATSR ANMAILS

_____

Word List

FOOD PANTRY • SHUT-INS • POOR
STRAY ANIMALS • BIRDS • HOMELESS

Jesus Walks on Water
Miracle (Matthew 14:22-33)

Name _____

Imagine you are Peter. You are in the boat with the other apostles. The wind is blowing and the waves are making the boat rock and bump. Then you see Jesus walking on the water toward you. Jesus calls you to come. Will you step out of the boat? Will you trust Jesus to keep you safe?

Sometimes it is not easy to trust God when you are afraid. That's when you should remember Peter's prayer. Solve the puzzle by taking the first letter of each picture clue and placing it in the blanks below. When you have solved the puzzle, you will know Peter's prayer by heart.

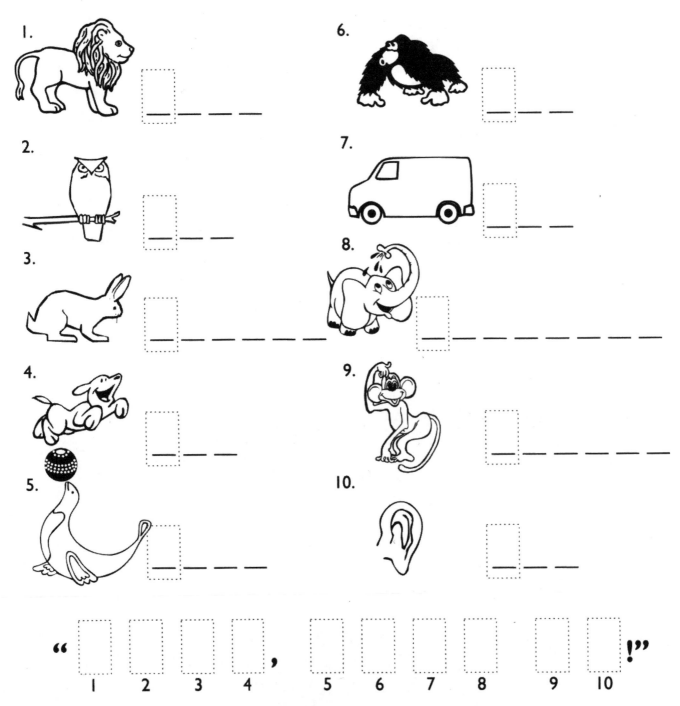

The Story of Bartimaeus

Miracle (Mark 10:46-52)

Bartimaeus believed that Jesus could give him his eyesight. Even when others told him to be quiet, the blind man did not give up calling. When Jesus told him to come forward, Bartimaeus was so excited he threw off his coat and ran. "I want to see again," he told Jesus. Jesus told him that he would see again. Jesus did not say, "I will make you well." He did not even say, "God will make you well." According to Jesus, what did make Bartimaeus well? Solve the rebus to discover the answer.

Work it out on this line. _____

Answer: ___ ___ ___ ___ ___

Who is cured in each of these stories from the Bible? Why does Jesus say each has been cured?

1. Matthew 15:22-28
• Who was cured?

_____

• Why? _____

_____

_____

2. Luke 17:11-19
• Who was cured?

_____

• Why? _____

_____

_____

3. Mark 2:3-12
• Who was cured?

_____

• Why? _____

_____

_____

Jesus Makes a Visit
Friendship (Luke 10:38-42)

Name _____

One day, Jesus and his followers came to a village called Bethany. In this village, there lived two sisters, Mary and Martha, who welcomed Jesus as a special guest in their home. Martha got busy fixing

something to eat for her guest, while Mary sat by Jesus and listened to him. After a while, Martha got tired of doing all the work. She even complained to Jesus that Mary was not helping her. Jesus said, "Martha, you are too worried about getting things done. Mary has really chosen the better part by spending time with me."

Answer these questions about this visit among friends. Use the word list if you need help.

1. In what town did this visit take place?

_____

2. Who is the special guest?

_____

3. What are the names of the two sisters?

_____

_____

4. Which sister was getting dinner ready for Jesus? _____

5. Which sister did Jesus say had chosen the "better part"? _____

6. What special thing did Mary do?

_____

Word List

Bethany

Mary and Martha

Listened to Jesus

Mary

Martha

Jesus

Something to think about and discuss...

• When you visit with your friends, what part of the visit do you most enjoy?

_____

_____

• Why? _____

_____

Called to Live Again
Friendship (John 11:1-44)

Name _____

Jesus loved his friends very much. When the brother of Mary and Martha died, Jesus saw how sad they were. He cried too. Then he did something wonderful. He call the man to come out of the tomb and return to life. Hidden in the puzzle below is the name of the man Jesus brought back to life. To solve the puzzle, first answer the clues and then write down the first letter of each answer on the blanks below.

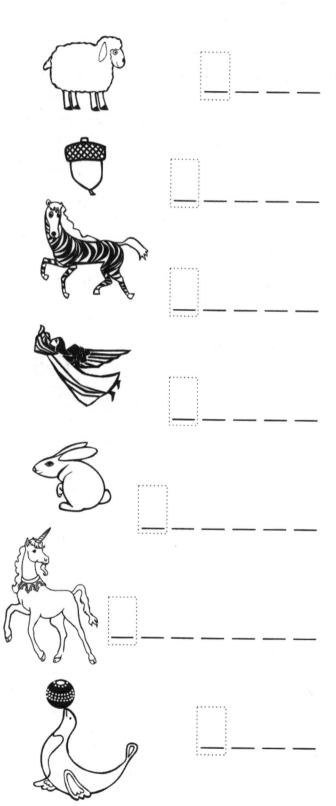

The brother of Mary and Martha
was named

☐ ☐ ☐ ☐ ☐ ☐ .

Jesus Arrives in Jerusalem
Palm Sunday (Mark 11:1-10)

Name _____

In the Bible story above, the people greet Jesus as he enters the city of Jerusalem. They spread palm branches before him and shout, "Hosanna! Blessed is the one who comes in the name of the Lord!" We can greet Jesus every day as he enters our hearts and our lives.

Make a palm-branch fan to remind yourself of how Jesus enters your own world every day. Trace the palm branch below. Make several copies. On each copy, write something you will do to honor Jesus. You can use your own ideas or borrow some from our list. Poke out the hole in each palm leaf, stack your leaves, and then insert a pronged fastener through the hole. Spread your leaves to make your fan.

Ways I Can Honor Jesus

Obey My Parents

Visit the Sick

Say a Prayer

Help a Neighbor

Be Cheerful

Share My Toys

Enjoy Nature

Thank God for Good Things

Go to Church

Make a Card for Someone

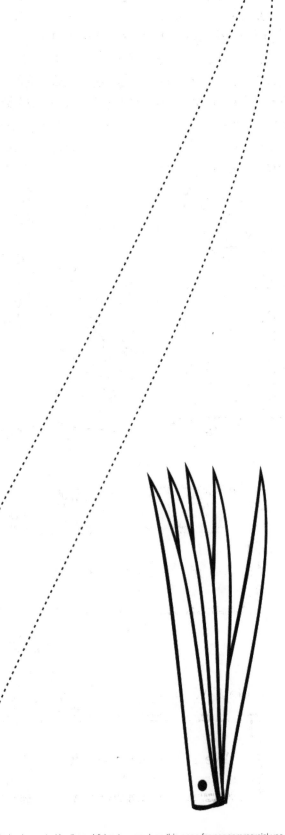

Jesus Has His Last Supper

Name _____

Holy Week (Matthew 26:17-29)

Have you ever been to a going-away party? It is a happy-sad time for everyone. It is a time to say, "Good-bye. I'll miss you." It is a time to say, "Thank you for being with me during this time," and "I'll never forget you." Jesus said all these things to his disciples at his Last Supper. He also gave us the gift of himself, a gift that keeps him with us always.

Solve the rebus to learn what Jesus' promise gift is called. Then unscramble the words below to complete Answer 2.

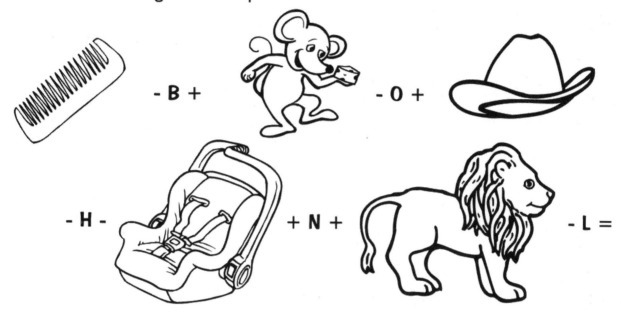

- B +   - O +

- H -   + N +   - L =

Work it out on this line. _____

Rebus Answer:

The gift Jesus left us is called Holy __ __ __ __ __ __ __ __ __ __ __.

REDBA   INEW

Scrambled Words Answer:

We can receive this gift as __ __ __ __ __ __ and __ __ __ __ __.

Betrayed! Arrested! Denied! Tried!

Name _____

Holy Week (Mark 14:43–15:5)

What a sad story we hear in the reading today. Using the reading and the Word List, complete the following quotes. Then think about and discuss the questions below with your classmates or family.

Word List

know • crucify • kiss
King • arrested

1. Judas said, "The one I will ___ ___ ___ ___ is the man" (Mark 14:44).

2. "Then they laid hands on him and

___ ___ ___ ___ ___ ___ ___ ___ him" (Mark 14:46).

3. Peter said, "I do not ___ ___ ___ ___ this man you

are talking about" (Mark 14:71).

4. Pilate said, "Are you the ___ ___ ___ ___ of the Jews?" (Mark 15:2)

5. The crowd shouted back,

"___ ___ ___ ___ ___ ___ ___ him!" (Mark 15:13)

Something to think about and discuss...

- Have you ever felt betrayed by a friend?

- Have you ever been accused of something you didn't do?

- What did you do about it? How did you feel?

Jesus Is Crucified
Holy Week (Mark 15:21-41)

Name _____

Then Jesus gave a loud cry and breathed his last.
And the curtain of the temple was torn in two, from top to bottom.
Mark 15:37,38

From all the things that happened when Jesus died on the cross, the people knew that he was truly God's Son. They remembered his teachings and his love. If you put the temple curtain together properly, you will discover many of the sayings of Jesus. Cut out the two sides of the curtain. Paste the curtain on a sheet of construction paper and hang the sayings of Jesus where you can read them every day.

ne another.
John 15:12

ve one another.
Luke 6:37

st you be judged.
Matthew 7:1

ur heavenly Father is perfect.
Matthew 5:48

ot worry.
Matthew 6:25

will be given to you.
Luke 11:19

ld have them do to you.
Matthew 7:12

will give you rest.
Matthew 11:28

ow me.
Matthew 4:19

e with you.
John 20:19

Love o
Forgi
Judge not le
Be perfect as yo
Do n
Ask, and it
Do to others as you wou
Come to me and I
Foll
Peace b

Jesus Lives!

Easter Sunday

(Matthew 28:8-15; John 20:11-18; Luke 24:13-35; Luke 24:35-48; John 21:1-14; Mark 16:9-14)

The stories of Easter are wonderful! Read any of the stories listed above and see why this is a day to be happy and celebrate. Then, using the pattern below, spread your Easter joy by making an Easter card for someone!

This is the day the Lord has made;

To _____

From _____

let us be glad!

Solutions to Selected Activities

"Well-come" Everyone! page 7
Cleansed, playful, refreshed, energized

Hear Their Stories, page 8
lectionary, sacramentary

Set the Table, page 9
1. altar
2. altar cloth
3. chalice
4. paten
5. cruets
6. ciborium

Prepare the Meal, page 10
The, altar, bread, Eucharist, Real, nourishes, Afterward, ciborium, lighted, everyone. TABERNACLE

Open the Door, page 11
1. We pray with the priest. God forgives our sins.
2. The door to God's love is open to you!

Signed and Sealed, page 14
1. believe
2. share
3. learn
4. succeed
5. receive

Hand in Hand, page 15
Peace I leave you,
My peace I give to you.
Peace be with you.

Love Glows On, page 16
1. rest
2. them
3. light
4. shine
5. souls
6. faithful
7. peace
8. Amen

Follow the "Cross Walk," page 18
The titles are in this order:
7, 2, 12, 5, 13, 8, 1, 6, 10, 14, 11, 9, 3, 4

A-maze-ing Incense, page 21
Loving God, hear our prayers.

Cross of Love, page 22
Love one another as I have loved you.

Light of Life, page 23
1. pray
2. assist
3. visit
4. help
5. teach
6. help
7. assist
8. have
9. pray

Many, Many Ministers, page 25

Moses, Man of God, page 28
Ten Commandments

Loving God Always, page 29
1. Prayers
2. Listen
3. Bible
4. church
5. Commandments
6. friends
7. thank you
8. afraid
9. decisions
10 gifts

Which Commandment? page 31
1. c
2. a
3. b
4. f
5. d
6. e

Which Is the Greatest? page 32
You shall love the Lord your God with all your heart and with all your soul and with all your mind.

A Circle of Love, page 33
As I have loved you.

Sermon on the Mount, page 35
1. heaven
2. comforted
3. earth
4. filled
5. mercy
6. God
7. children

What It Means to Be Blessed, page 36
Clues: goat, beaver, bunny, whale, wheel, birds, tire, barn
Answer: Your reward is great in heaven

A Chance to Choose, page 38
Across: 3. cheating, 4. stealing, 5. anger
Down: 1. disobedience, 2. lying

A Special Bonus, page 41
Whatever you do for others, you do for me.

Doing Good, page 42
1. f
2. g
3. b
4. e
5. a
6. d
7. c

Praying for Others, page 43.
1. Convert the sinner.
2. Instruct the ignorant.
3. Counsel the doubtful.
4. Comfort the sorrowful.
5. Bear wrongs patiently.
6. Forgive all injuries.
7. Pray for the living and the dead.

Playing Fair, page 44

Treat everyone as you want to be treated.

Fixing the Circle of Love, page 46
Note: Give students examples for *repair:* return what was taken; fix or replace what was broken.

Be a Peacemaker, page 47
Words: heart, foot, face, dollar, coffee, peach
Answer: The peace of the Lord

Two Special Sacraments, page 48
FORK – K + GEAR – EAR + FIVE – F + NEST – T + S = FORGIVENESS
SUN – S + KITE + Y – KEY + Y = UNITY

God's Loving Creation, page 53
moon, stars, at night, sun, gives, light, fish, seas, birds, trees, animals, us, loves us all

Creation Word Search, page 54

A Sad Story, pages 57-58
1. littered
2. poisons, junk
3. killed
4. cut down
5. lived
6. smoke
7. weapons
8. disrespect
9. plan

I Can Help, page 60
Water: saving, turn off, showers, litter, poisoning
Air: conserve, smoke, walk, riding, heat, pollution

Saving the Trees, page 62
recycle newspapers, reuse grocery bags, plant trees and gardens

How Can We Save the Animals? pages 63-64
Instruct the children to color the pages and cut the "window" on page 1 as indicated. If you have not copied the pages back to back, have the children paste, staple, or tape them together and fold to make a booklet.

Saying No to Bad Habits, page 66
drugs, cigarettes, alcohol, junk food, healthy, exercise

Caring for God's Creation, page 68

Mary and the Angel, page 71
Angel: You will have a son and name him Jesus.
Mary: I will do as God asks of me.

Jesus Is Born, page 72
Across: 2. Bethlehem, 4. inn, 5. Christmas, 7. Mary, 9. donkey, 10, Joseph, 11. stable
Down: 1. Holy Family, 3. manger, 6. innkeeper, 8. Augustus

Messengers from Heaven, page 73
Clues: ghost, heart, girl, dog, hive, teeth, stone, yarn
Answer: Glory to God in the highest heaven.

Star Search, pages 74-75

Keeping Jesus Safe, page 76
1. King Herod
2. Jerusalem
3. The Wise Men
4. Bethlehem

5. Egypt
6. Nazareth

Little Boy Lost, page 77
Clues: fan, sunshine, thumb, tire, toys, men, bees
Answer: I must be in my Father's house.

Jesus and the Devil, page 78
1. C
2. A
3. E
4. B
5. D

Naming the Twelve, page 79

Bonus Questions: Judas, Peter, James and John, Andrew and Simon Peter

Jesus and the Children, page 80
Clues: corn, moon, teeth, moth, child, heel, reel
Answer: Let the children come to me.

The Lesson at Cana, page 81
Do what Jesus tells you.

Jesus Cures a Little Girl, page 82
She is not dead, but sleeping.

Jesus Feeds the Hungry, page 83
poor, birds, food pantry, homeless, shut-ins, stray animals

Jesus Walks on Water, page 84
Clues:
1. lion
2. owl
3. rabbit
4. dog
5. seal
6. ape
7. van
8. elephant
9. monkey
10. ear
Answer: Lord, save me!

The Story of Bartimaeus, page 85
FOX – OX + PAIL – P + DOG – D – LOG + BATH +
LL – BALL = FAITH

Jesus Makes a Visit, page 86
1. Bethany
2. Jesus
3. Mary and Martha
4. Martha
5. Mary
6. Listened to Jesus

Called to Live Again, page 87
Clues: lamb, acorn, zebra, angel, rabbit, unicorn, seal
Answer: Lazarus

Jesus Has His Last Supper, page 89
COMB – B + MOUSE – O + HAT – H – SEAT + N +
LION – L = COMMUNION
Rebus answer: Communion
Scrambled words answer: bread, wine

Betrayed! Arrested! Denied! Tried! page 90
1. kiss
2. arrested
3. know
4. King
5. crucify

Jesus Lives! page 92
Give each child a folded piece of 8 ½ x 11
construction paper. After the children color their egg
patterns, have them paste their eggs on the folded
paper. Inside, have them write a joyful message of their
own.